AF801072

Positive Financial Behavior:

A Motivational Guide

Debbie J. Slaughter

© Debbie J. Slaughter 2022

This work is subject to copyright. All rights are reserved by the author worldwide, whether the whole or part of the material concerned, specifically the rights of translation, reprinting, recitation, broadcasting, reproduction on microfilms or in any other physical way, and transmission or information storage and retrieval, electronic adaption, or by similar or dissimilar methodology now known or hereafter developed. None of this publication may be republished in any form by any means, including photocopying, scanning or otherwise without prior written permission to the copyright holder.

Paperback: 978-0-578-38746-8

INTRODUCTION

The journey described in this body of work is special because I am writing from personal experience and what I have learned through my education and training. I am very passionate about practicing positive financial behaviors, but it is not something that I have practiced all my life. I wasn't taught personal finance in school or at home. Like many of you, I am from the era of "mom/dad, can I have this?" "No." "Why?" "Cause I said so." Finances were simply not discussed. We grew up needing to figure it out on our own, which is ok; but at what point do we learn positive financial behaviors?

Most of us don't know where our financial behaviors come from or how to develop them in a positive way. I genuinely believe that achieving your financial goals starts with looking at your behaviors. In chapter one, I challenge you to look within and acknowledge your current financial behaviors. I believe that understanding begins with inward reflection and aligning yourself with your financial purpose.

Every goal is different, everyone's financial journey is unique, and the outcome varies for every individual with set goals. What may work for someone may not work for you because your financial behavior is different. For example, two people may have the same plan of paying off a debt, but the journey to get there is different because both individuals have different incomes, needs, lifestyles, habits, and patterns.

The objective of this book is to help you reflect on your current behaviors, identify the behavior (or behaviors) that you want to redirect in a more positive direction, and motivate you to work toward positive financial behaviors.

My journey to learning about my financial behaviors and then redirecting them didn't happen overnight. I wasn't raised knowing what debt was or how to save, or even how to invest. Finances weren't a part of our daily family discussions. I didn't get finance lessons at school. I learned the same way most adults learn about adulting; winging it. I was hired for a position that had a financial counselor in-office. I always had a passion for personal finance but things didn't align for me until I landed this position as an administrative assistant. My supervisor encouraged my desire to learn and they paid for my first course: Money Management Essentials through the AFCPE program. Once I finished that, they paid for my Certified Credit Report Reviewer materials. I passed that test and then I paid for Military Essentials through AFCPE and received that designation. I couldn't stop at this point. I paid for and received my Certified Financial Education Instructor designation. One day I checked my spam mail and noticed that I received a scholarship. It wasn't supposed to go to my spam mail, it was a legitimate scholarship and I paid for my Accredited Financial Counselor designation. It seems as though my life was finally aligned to allow me to throw myself into the field I was always so passionate about. I'm most certainly not finished. There is still a lot I want to learn and do, and financial goals that I want to set for myself. Each journey requires a new behavioral direction.

This book is not a how-to guide. I will not write about how to save X amount of dollars to reach $50k by the end of the year. I am not going to teach you how much and where to invest. By reading my book, I hope you gain a better understanding of your financial behavior and find some motivation to reach your financial goals. This way, we can change the dialogue from "Because I said so." to "It's just not in my budget right now, but maybe you can work toward saving enough to buy it yourself." When you understand, you practice; when you practice, you learn, and as you learn, you educate. Please enjoy!

CHAPTER 1

ALIGNMENT AND REFLECTION

Much like working out or running a new business, the most challenging part of any new journey is starting. Before you start on your financial quest, I encourage you to learn more about your current behaviors and your habits. When you can identify what practices haven't worked so well for your particular goals, you'll know precisely what behaviors need tweaking and what a positive direction looks like for that specific behavior. Being transparent with yourself and your behavior toward how you use money is challenging. It's easy to say, "Well, this is what has worked for me in the past, so I'm going to keep doing it," even though it doesn't align with your financial goal. That's not to say it's "bad" behavior, but is it helping you achieve the financial goals you have set for yourself? Sometimes we set goals and turn to savings challenges or books on how to make millions on investments. You can read books, but some things may not resonate with you because it doesn't speak to your current financial situation. All we know is that the bills have to get paid. So how do we start converting these behaviors that aren't working with your financial goal into behaviors that are?

Before I continue, I want you to re-read the above paragraph with a little more purpose. Notice that I purposefully did not say “change” (I prefer redirecting) or “bad behavior ."Positive behavior, with anything in life, starts with a positive mentality. I don't believe there are "bad" choices, but there are choices that you make in everyday life that take you further away from your goals. Your finances are specifically yours, so you are the only one in the way of your dreams.

There are ways to get the things that you want without that feeling of guilt, regret, and doubt. First, you will have to practice patience. If you are impatient with your finances, this is where you look at yourself in the mirror, acknowledge it, and think about ways to learn patience so that you start practicing positive financial behavior. The act of wanting is not bad behavior but making a stress-related or emotional purchase when you can't afford it might put you in a temporary bind. That stress/emotional energy is what you want to pinpoint when thinking about redirection.

You won't lose your house by buying a new pair of shoes. But, this is where living paycheck to paycheck is rooted. If you decide to bypass the shoes one weekend because you are trying to "be good," then you decide to go out with friends the following weekend; what you have done was simply shift your funds from one impulse buy to the other, but it's still the same financial behavior. You may have even thought, "I was good last week because I didn't buy the shoes, so I deserve something this week!" But you didn't save any additional money for this something. You're essentially spending the same money for the outing that you would have spent on the shoes. I'm not saying you can't have these things, but you have to be conscious about how and when you make these purchases so that you can budget accordingly. Waiting until all the bills have been paid and money transferred to my savings before buying something for myself has worked well for me in the past.

Even then, I waited until a few days before I got paid again to spend money on variable expenses. When I do this, I have peace of mind knowing that everything is taken care of; and if something pops up, I have already transferred money to my savings for that reason.

Putting your positive financial behaviors into practice takes time, and well, PRACTICE! There are things that you have to learn along the way for your financial toolbox. However, the little bumps and bruises that you have already felt along your journey into adulthood should be more than enough to get you started. Once you have been honest with yourself about your current spending habits, then the process of redirecting can begin. It doesn't stop there, however. You may not get it right the first time, or the second, or maybe not even the third time. But, if you are dedicated enough to make the shift toward positive financial behavior, and you believe enough in yourself that you will make that shift, you will reach your financial goals and live peacefully with your finances.

It will be discouraging when you see that you repeat the behaviors you're trying to redirect. When you don't reach a goal that you set for yourself, it's disheartening. As humans, we all have decisions to make, and they may not always be the ones that lead you to your financial goal. Sometimes you have to pay for something which diverts your intentions on saving money. When this happens, it can take you out of alignment. It becomes a test. Will you let this challenge stop you from reaching your financial goals? It's in this moment where you have to be the most forgiving with yourself. Allow yourself the time to handle this "something" that you have to pay for while thinking of ways to realign your strategy to achieve your financial goal. Positive financial behaviors start a positive mindset.

It can be challenging to maneuver through an obstacle. The key is to manage the situation tactfully to make positive changes in our lives. The first step on your road to financial reform is admitting that change is necessary. Once you've acknowledged the need for change, it's time for some honest reflection. What are your spending habits? Do you have any debts that are causing you stress? How much money do you currently have saved for emergencies and retirement? What way of thinking or money management technique is steering you away from your financial goals?

Once you clearly understand your current financial situation, it will be easier to create goals and develop a plan of action. However, don't worry – this process doesn't have to be daunting! With a bit of self-reflection and some guidance, you'll be on your way to making methodical financial decisions.

Reflect on your wants and needs

When making financial decisions, you first need to be very honest about your desires (new car or shopping) and needs (transportation and clothes). Your desire for a new car or expensive clothes can cloud the need for transportation and clothing. The former needs redirection until you have become more conscious of your financial behavior. You need to be honest with yourself about what you need in life. By reflecting on your wants and needs, you can start asking yourself what you want in life and how money can help you achieve those things?

The more you understand your wants and needs, the easier it will be to make sound financial decisions that align with what is important to you. The mind is a powerful tool, so use it to your advantage when making decisions about your money.

Know the difference between wants and needs

Many think the concept of wants versus needs is simple, but not understanding the difference comes from childhood. For example, most children can't sleep without their favorite stuffed animal. They need this stuffed animal to go to bed, find it first thing in the morning and play with it throughout the day. If they don't have it, they can't sleep. They need this stuffed animal, but it is actually a want. The attachment to this item feels like a need, but it’s not. We grow up attached to toys and stuffed animals, and we associate it with needing and are never told that it's not a need. Food, shelter, and clothing are needs. As adults, we still have these childlike desires for things that we think we need. Keep in mind that your wants are desires. One needs food, but they want steak. It's hard to decipher this concept because food is a necessity; therefore, it's easy to justify overspending on food, one, because we're hungry and, two, the convenience of purchasing it. If something isn't a necessity, it is a luxury and should be treated as such. When you start identifying whether purchases are wants or needs, it's easier to make well-thought-out financial decisions.

Figure out your values

Your values should guide the decisions you make about money. What is important to you? It helps to understand where your values lie, so we better understand where our money is going. We spend money on things we value most. Opening a savings account specifically for travel or variable expenses would be an excellent strategy to avoid putting it on credit or overspending. Setting up a secondary savings account for hobbies would be a good strategy also, but having a small limit store card could also be beneficial if they offer rewards and discounts. For example, you charge supplies to your store card but then pay it off quickly with the funds from the designated savings account.

Your values are the linchpin of all your financial decisions, so it's vitally important that you figure out what they are and use them when making these decisions. When you do this, you will be more inclined to make sound choices because they align with your values.

Know how much money you have

It might seem like common sense, but many people don't understand that the money they bring home isn't 100% theirs. At the beginning of each month, take some time to look at your net income and make a list of your debts. Then, make a list of your necessary expenses (utilities, cable/internet, cellphone, childcare, etc.). Anything left over is how much money you have. Checking your account balance regularly can help you make smarter decisions about how and when you spend your money.

By reflecting on what you want in life, figuring out your values, knowing how much money you have, differentiating between wants and needs, creating a budget, and treating each dollar as valuable, you can make smarter choices with your money.

When it comes to making positive financial decisions, no matter what stage of life you're in, it's essential to reflect on what is going well and where there might be room for improvement. This process of self-reflection allows you to become aware of your behaviors when it comes to finances which then helps you recognize the behavior or behaviors that need to be redirected in a more positive direction. When this happens, you will work toward making positive financial decisions that align with their values by being more intentional about your spending habits and better prepared for any obstacle you encounter.

Reflecting on Your Current Financial Behavior

Before making any changes to your financial choices, take some time every month to reflect and think about the decisions you make every day. Is everything going as planned? What is working well, and what needs improvement? When it comes to making positive financial decisions, the first step is determining if your lifestyle aligns with your financial goals. This requires you to be honest with yourself and become aware of your daily habits. Are you in alignment? Once you have a firm understanding of where you are in alignment with your goals, it will be easier for you to change your behavior in healthier ways to help you achieve everything you have set for yourself.

Start by finding a quiet place with minimal distractions where you can sit down and spend fifteen minutes thinking about your values, lifestyle, goals, and how your relationship with money is getting you closer toward OR pulling you further away from these values and goals. Consider the following questions:

- What are my values when it comes to money?
- Is everything going as planned with my income and expenses? Are you living within your means?
- What would financial independence look like for me?
- Are your bills getting paid? If not, why not?
- Which of these goals can be achieved through better financial habits?

Once you have completed this exercise, write down your responses and reflections. Again, be patient with yourself but be very honest. These answers will help give you have a clearer idea of what needs to change to redirect your behavior in a more positive direction, which leads to improved financial health overall.

These questions require deep thought about who you are, what is important to you, and where you want to be financially. This reflection period should be uninterrupted time to yourself, so give yourself some time to reflect by yourself or with a partner you share financial goals with (spouse or business partner) and be honest, but be kind and forgiving. You can't go into a positive direction in life or financially by starting out dishonest and unforgiving.

Even if you think you have everything planned out, spending some time thinking about these things will lead to significant discoveries about how your life and financial goals align with your financial behavior.

There are no right or wrong answers when considering a journey with money because this is an intensely personal process that only you can navigate and control. You have complete control. Your financial situation might change over time according to external factors like changes in career, marriage, children, etc. Still, this self-reflection process reveals what is truly important at this specific point in your life. Knowing yourself, accepting the financial habits that aren't in alignment with your financial goals, and redirecting those behaviors toward achieving what you want, allow you to make positive choices.

Reflect on our past spending habits and see where we can improve

Reflecting on our spending habits is essential in making better financial decisions. Learning about spending triggers can help us understand what patterns we practice that need to be redirected. Asking ourselves these questions might also encourage us to reflect on how we feel about money and how it makes us feel when we misspend it. From personal experience, I noticed that I did more online window shopping the days leading up to payday. I had an urge to buy something, and I had to identify if I wanted to buy it because I had the money left over from the previous pay period or did I want to buy it because I had money coming in. Once I noticed this trend, I redirected that urge to spend money and applied it to paying down my car loan. My thought process: had I spent money on something online rather than putting more toward my goal, I wouldn't be in alignment with my goals and putting myself further away from achieving it rather than closer.

So when you get these urges to spend money, as I had, write it down, if possible, or make a mental note and have the conversation with yourself. This will help you visualize a clearer picture of your current spending habits, your honest thoughts about money, when you feel these urges, and how you can realign your financial behavior with your financial goals.

How do I currently think about money?

"Finance is not merely about making money. It's about achieving our deep goals and protecting the fruits of our labor. It's about stewardship and, therefore, about achieving the good society." – Robert J. Shiller

If you don't know where to start in your self-reflecting journey, ask yourself the following questions: keep in mind these are suggestions to guide you.

Does spending money give me anxiety? Does spending money give me a thrill? Do I not care either way?

What do I think is enough money?

What are my spending triggers? How does this align with my goals?

You should ask yourself to get a better idea of your relationship with money.

Money is fleeting, and we're trying to beat the buzzer.

Money is a sensitive subject for many people. We all have to deal with it as adults, and we use it every day. Familiarizing yourself with positive financial behavior and sound money management should be important to your daily life. The more you know about finances, the more confident you'll feel at reaching your goals and making changes to your life. Think of money management as a game. The more you understand the rules, the more you practice positive financial behavior, the better you will manage your finances, and the easier it will become to win the game. Of course, you will lose games sometimes, but you have to keep playing to get better and leave that lasting legacy for those after you.

Although there are books and programs and blogs about money management, there isn't much out there that caters to the individual reader about their own plans and journey pertaining to money. Not everybody's blessing is the same. There is no one way to achieve your goal. It’s easy to say, "I'm going to stop using credit cards/I'm going to stop spending on unnecessary things /I'm going to start saving more of my money," but it is not that easy to do it. Why? I may have come up with a few reasons for you:

- Our culture is very credit-driven. Instant gratification takes priority over future planning and reward.
- It can be challenging to get out of our routines or habits. Even though we know that they are no good for us in the end, it is hard to stop doing them just like that.
- Habits are difficult to break because they have become part of our personalities over time.

Fortunately, if you have at least one of these reasons in your self-reflection, there are some actionable steps you can take right now to help you redirect those behaviors.

Treat each dollar as valuable.

"Spend Money wisely, you can either make yourself or break yourself when you got money in hand."

— Tono Williams

The amount of money you earn does not matter if you do not treat it with respect. Every dollar is valuable and we should think of our finances in that way. By treating every dollar like it has significant value, people can make better choices about their money, leading to improved financial situations. You may have bought an item on sale, plus an additional discount, and found $20 that you had forgotten about in your pocket, but where are the funds for that purchase MOST valuable? In your savings account? Putting additional money on your debt? Set aside for a nice gift or a family trip? "BUT IT'S ON SALE, AND IT HAS AN ADDITIONAL DISCOUNT, AND I FOUND $20!!!! I NEED THIS! This deal doesn't come around very often!" I can promise you it does. Maybe not the additional $20, but the deal will come around several times in the year. It'll just be advertised differently. This is the moment when you need to stop and think and write down your thought process. Where is the money most valuable? If you have reached your monthly savings contribution goal or your debt reduction goal, and you're satisfied with your planning and finances, go ahead and spend the money. But not before giving it some serious thought and being honest with yourself.

If you have evaluated your behaviors and you still can't quite figure out a plan of action, it may be time to seek financial counseling from an accredited counselor. They can help you look at your finances and give you some ideas that will work for your unique situation.

It is also important to mention three things:

- If you want to see positive changes in your finances, you must commit yourself to it 100%. We cannot make any excuses when following through with our goals. This one was difficult for me because I felt like there was always something. There will always be something. Stay committed!

Money requires constant attention and self-reflection because its influence over us is strong; if we want to have a better relationship with it, we need to take the time to think about our current financial behaviors and improve on them.

If you can be patient and not expect quick rewards, you will be able to create a healthier money management system for yourself that will allow you to spend your hard-earned money (or maybe even make more money) more deliberately without feeling restricted or like you're missing out on something.

Maybe you need to downsize or change your lifestyles

Changing your lifestyle to accommodate your financial status will yield great reward. Downsizing is a great way to hit the replay button. You can identify where your values lie and learn about your behavior in the process, which makes for wiser upsizing.

Alternately, we all have been in situations where we did not have much money and had to "get by." Perhaps you are currently facing a similar situation. Legendary tennis player Mr. Arthur Ashe said, "Start where you are…Use what you have…Do what you can…." Sometimes that is all you need. Start with what you have and do what you can with that. If you do this and practice positive financial behavior, you will reach your goals even when bumps in the road try to stop you. Everyone is capable and deserving of the lifestyle they desire; it just takes work.

Signs that you need to redirect your financial behavior:

* There comes a point when every individual has met their threshold for how much they need to survive day-to-day. If you feel you have reached a threshold or are close, it might be time for reflection, alignment, and possibly financial counseling.* No matter how much you make, financial control is possible.

* You may not have enough money to pay all of your bills.*

* You feel a constant sense of stress about money that never seems to go away.*

* When you find yourself borrowing from one creditor to pay another creditor.*

* When you feel the urge to spend and act on impulse*

Your bills are paid, and your savings is satisfactory, but you want to travel or purchase a home and can never seem to find the extra money to save for it You're stagnant.

If you find yourself in any of these situations, a little talk with yourself about what can or needs to change will open many doors.

Starting a savings account for different events helps alleviate a lot of the stress because you are now better equipped to make the necessary purchases. Putting money aside for an emergency, a separate account in the event of a career transition, and one for things that happen once a year (birthdays, anniversaries, holidays, etc.) is good practice for positive financial behavior. The latter is not a surprise since it happens once every year, so there is no reason it should be put on credit every year and take you months to pay off. Saving for this now will alleviate a lot of stress.

As you reflect on the above paragraph, ask yourself: What is the **one** change you could make to your current financial behaviors or habits in order to mediate the above-mentioned financial stressors? What is the one thing you can redirect to be better prepared? I had to write all of my fixed bills out and know the exact day it was deducted from my account. NOT the day they bill me or the day it was a pending charge, but the exact day it posts to my account. This way, I know when that particular bill is coming out of my check. The billing date is different than the day you are charged, so be mindful of this and ensure that you have enough funds in your account to cover this transaction. It has happened to me several times, and this knowledge of my funds has made a considerable impact.

What steps can you take TODAY toward making change happen? Write it down and put it somewhere you will see it every day until it becomes a habit.

Saving money is a mindset.

"He becometh poor that worketh with a slack hand; But the hand of the diligent maketh rich." – Proverbs 10:4

In this book, you will gain a different perspective on making better financial decisions and insight into identifying your current behaviors. By learning how to take control of your mind and emotions, you can begin saving money immediately.

The first step is recognizing that saving money takes a lot of self-control and discipline. It requires patience and accepting that things won't always go as planned. You must be willing to push yourself outside of your comfort zone to acquire the skills and behaviors that allow you to reach your financial goals. This process includes being very honest with yourself about why you spend, where you are spending (not "where" as in location but does your money go towards hair care products or sporting goods or restaurants, etc.), as well as identifying the feeling before, during, and after this urge purchase.

The best way to improve your financial situation is by redirecting those habits that drain your bank account. Start putting your goals first instead of constantly spending money on yourself or other people or things that do not benefit you as a person. If the action does not align with your goals, such as saving for college or retirement, it does not benefit you to waste your time. And time is MONEY! I know this sounds selfish, but it's important to think about your future and the future of any dependents who rely on you financially, such as children and aging parents.

Learn how to develop new habits and stick with them until they become second nature so that you can begin to save money month after month without even thinking about it! This takes time, so be patient with yourself. Remember that positive reinforcement is key to staying motivated. Celebrate your wins, no matter how small they may seem, and learn from your mistakes along the way. I have learned over the years that simple changes lead to long-term success.

CHAPTER 2

COMMITMENT

"Success is never found. Failure is never fatal. Courage is the only thing." Winston Churchill

It is easier to decide on a pair of shoes and commit to purchasing those shoes. To decide on a healthier lifestyle and commit to it. For some, choosing a partner and committing to the relationship may come with some ease. However, for some reason, committing to a financially conscious lifestyle does not come as easy. More expensive purchases involve credit scores, impulse buys are typically pointless items we don't need, and unforeseen expenses come with headaches and possible financial ruin. Oppressing your desires for things, improving your credit score, preparing for the unexpected, all the while paying off debt, and doing all of this simultaneously is a marathon—a long journey of change, discipline, and redirection. However, there is a way to save money, pay off debt, and not sacrifice your fun or lifestyle. Just like working out, you have to do things in moderation. You have to decide to pull back and commit to bettering your financial situation.

It took me a long time to dedicate my life to understanding the ins and outs of finances. Learning and understanding personal finance was always a passion of mine, but when I tried to implement it, there was always something that hindered my progress. It is so hard to decide to do something about your financial situation because as soon as you make this decision, and things are smooth sailing, all of a sudden, your check engine light comes on, or something happens, and there goes $1500 from your savings! It is incredibly frustrating. Most of us relieve this stress by retail therapy, food therapy, or adult beverage therapy, all of which come at a high cost and some regret afterward.

Before you decide to commit to your financial goals, you need to understand that a change needs to be made to reach this goal and prepare yourself with the financial knowledge to achieve it.

How do we get ourselves motivated? Setting goals is exciting, but long-term commitment can make you feel unmotivated. Each step that you take either brings you closer to your version of success or pulls you farther away from it; either way, you will continue to head in the direction of your financial behavior/pattern.

The first step is acknowledging that you need to redirect your financial situation

The first step to changing your current financial situation is acknowledging and identifying which behavior needs redirecting. In the case of being financially unstable, this means admitting that you may have been living off of debt because your behavior is above your means (income). On the other hand, it could be the complete opposite. You may be living off of debt because you have money hoarding tendencies. You have the money in your checking or savings or stashed away somewhere, but you refuse to use it. You may prefer to use a credit card because it's not your money, and when it's time to make payments, you like that it's only a little at a time because you don't want to "waste" your money.

Having debt is not a bad thing. Debt is actually good if it's managed correctly. You need a good mix of installment loans and revolving loans. All you need to show lenders and creditors is that you can manage your debt well by making on-time payments and having consistent utilization. If you are mismanaging debt, maybe your approach to debt management is the behavior should be redirected toward managing debt better. In which case, your goal might be managing debt properly. Redirection here may look like shifting the way you feel about debt and making it a priority so that you can enjoy your income once everything is paid off.

Commit to understanding the value of your funds.

People can make more informed spending decisions when they understand their behavior regarding opportunity costs. Your financial outlook can change by gaining insight into what you currently spend money on. Opportunity cost is something a person bypasses for the benefit of another purchase. For example, you forego purchasing a sweater in the winter for school books for your class. You sacrifice going out to eat for lunch for bringing your lunch. Think about opportunity cost when you commit to improving your financial decision-making process based on your behavior. Make sure you do more research on this concept.

By understanding opportunity cost, you begin to see how to redirect to improve your financial situation. One of the best ways to track past opportunity cost decisions is to go back into your account. What did you buy at Target? What did you sacrifice for that purchase? By monitoring daily expenses -the fixed expenses as well as the variables- it becomes easier to identify patterns in behavior that help you identify the impulse spending versus the necessary spending.

If you find that a particular behavior consistently drains your account balance, then it would be wise for you to redirect those wasteful activities. When funds are low, consider your variable expenses because they are the most flexible.

Commit to REDIRECTION | Same habit, different allocation

It is human nature to want things to stay the same. For those looking at ways to make more positive financial decisions, you have to commit to reaching your financial goals and redirecting your habits. Very little will happen if you continue with the same financial habits that have not allowed you to reach your desired outcome.

This "change" may be replacing one behavior with another – but it's something different and therefore may yield a better reward than the outcome your previous behavior attributed. It's like deciding that instead of eating fast food every day, you're going to eat half as much fast food and twice as many meal-prepped meals every day. You haven't stopped eating; you've just reduced the amount of money spent on eating fast food. You've substituted a financial behavior for a slightly better positive financial behavior. This is the sort of "behavior modification" that will allow you to reach your financial goals in most situations.

To redirect your financial behavior, you must first identify the deciding factors with each purchase in your current financial behavior that puts you further away from your goal. It's been said before, but it bears repeating: self-reflection is a necessary component in any change we wish to create within ourselves. Acknowledgment and self-reflection are the first steps, but the commitment to shifting your financial behavior shouldn't be taken lightly. Commitment is serious. It means you are making something or someone else a priority. Your financial goals and dreams should be a priority. Self-care and financial care are priorities because you may not be the only one depending on you or your finances.

Make a list of your current behaviors and their accompanying outcomes

Write down everything that you have spent money on necessarily or frivolously; things that have lasted a month and will continue to last, and things that have lasted a few days and no longer add value. I also encourage you to make a sidenote of why you purchased it and how it made you feel. For example, did you buy it cause you were stressed? Starving? Out of necessity? To impress?

After you have done this, organize these behaviors into two lists: behaviors that are currently hurting your financial situation and behaviors that you consider to be at least somewhat helpful to your current financial state.

If possible, try to organize this list in terms of the most hurtful on the left side and the least affected, financially, on the right. Kind of like a pros and cons list! Everyone loves a good pros and cons list. You can even do it in order of severity – the behavior or pattern that pulls you away from your goal the most, and then the intermediate behavior, and lastly, least goal-deterring behavior.

Once you have your list complete, look at the cons and figure out what you can do financially to change the behavior so that you can still do that con but in a positive way financially. You may have to wait longer to get what you want because your goal is to save for it and pay cash. If it's a minor purchase (and you're good at managing your credit card), put it on credit and pay it off quickly. I sincerely believe that you can have everything you want; you just have to be patient and analytical about how you obtain it and ensure that the money is working for you and not against you.

After evaluating your list and identifying ways to redirect your behavior, it's time to commit—genuine commitment without waiver.

Find the motivation that will push you through any obstacle.

For change in your financial behavior to happen, there must be a desire within you for a better or more stable financial situation. It has to come from inside; an external motivator is not enough. You can't wait around until something, or someone, makes you do what needs to be done. You have to be your motivator. You need to set goals for yourself and make them specific, measurable, achievable, relevant, and time-bound. Having clear goals will motivate you to commit and do what it takes to realize them because they provide direction (Relevant), motivation (Achievable), and accountability (Time-Bound).

So take some time now to set some SMART financial goals that will guide the changes you want to make in your life.

Make a plan - what do you need to do to improve your financial situation?

Take action - start by identifying the behavior you want to redirect and figure out how you will be purposeful in shifting that energy to achieve your goal. Commit!!

CHAPTER 3

DILIGENCE AND OVERCOMING OBSTACLES

"We don't have to be smarter than the rest. We have to be more disciplined than the rest." – Warren Buffet

Many financial experts would agree that most people need to do three things: spend less than they earn, invest their savings, and manage debt wisely.

You may already know this, but it's important to remember: Financial discipline does not mean depriving yourself of what you want. Being financially disciplined means identifying what behaviors are not supporting your financial goals and making the necessary redirection to achieve them. Financial discipline means staying committed to yourself and your finances. Stay committed to your journey and your way of doing things. Don't look around and see what everybody else did to reach the same goal you have. If you want a particular job, you're not going to go out and buy the same outfit someone else wore who got the same position. You're going to look your best. You're going to answer the questions in the interview your way. If you want to work out, you're not going to steal the car of someone you saw going to the gym. That car isn't going to put you on the same path to weight loss as the owner of the vehicle took. You're going to exercise your way. You're going to eat in such a way that benefits your physical goals. If you are on a spiritual journey, you're not going to read the same book as someone who has obtained the level of spirituality that you want to achieve. You're more inclined to read a book for your level of interest and the guidance that best fits your situation. All of this is the same with finances. Follow your path, correct your behaviors and create your own lane.

I don't want you to view financial disciplines and commitment as negative or restricting. Instead, view them as stepping stones in the right direction! Take a moment to think about your next steps and stay committed and diligent. This chapter provides some suggestions to help you financially disciplined, but you must craft your plan for financial discipline.

Be mindful every time you spend money

Being financially disciplined is about spending less than you earn and being mindful of your spending habits and triggers. It means having the self-control to think about the goal before making an impulse buy or going on an emotional whim. Spend within, or below, your means so that you can accumulate savings over time.

Through my studies in financial counseling, I learned about money hoarders and avoiders. Money hoarders like to make money and never touch it. They make the most minimum payments because they don't want to see money leave their account. Avoiders do just that; they avoid making payments, avoid saving, but they spend like it's no tomorrow. Knowing which kind of money manager you are will help you in your journey to positive financial behaviors and improve your decision-making process.

To avoid spending too much money, wait until after all of the bills and debts have been paid, then put some in your savings, and THEN whatever is left is your spending money. I had a habit of thinking about things I wanted to purchase with my next check before it had even arrived. So, when I got paid, I would spend money on something I wanted and then I paid the bills. Unfortunately, my savings didn't grow very much. When I tried to do things with the family, or travel, or save for a goal, I found myself either unable to or taking longer to do these things because the money was already misplaced before I had gotten paid. So I had to redirect my energy and behavior from thinking about what I wanted to buy with my next check to "let me wait until everything is paid and I'll use whatever is left. Doing this worked for me because it showed me that I could grow my savings and that I really wanted to put the extra money towards debt to pay it off quicker. This small choice to wait until later actually shifted my behavior on its own. I realized that I liked waiting until everything was paid first and then I noticed that my behavior shifted naturally toward paying off debt.

After that, I was mindful of my purchases. I started to ask myself, "how can I purchase this so that my goals are still a priority?" I was committed to my goal and purposeful with my funds. When you are diligent, everything somehow aligns and just works. When you put your attention on the financial matters that require it, the stress and anxiety go away, and you somehow have enough to do all the things you want to do and buy whatever it is you want to buy. But you have to make the decision to align and commit.

"The thoughts of the diligent tend only to plenteousness; but of everyone that is hasty to want." – Proverbs 21:5

Learning more about personal finance and how it works will greatly assist your financial endeavors. Learning about how credit works, reading your credit report, different savings methods that might work for your goal, and how and when to invest are just some of the things that will help along the way.

You can spend money on what you want. It's all about timing

I don't like when people say, "I was bad this weekend and bought XYZ." I don't think people should omit things that they want. I also don't think people should feel bad about buying something. There is a way to have what you want and reach your financial goals. You may have to postpone the purchase until you have the money saved to pay it with cash. If you are about to get paid in the next few days, you might be able to put it on credit and pay it off quickly once it posts/when you get paid. The misconception about purchasing on credit is that the best way to show good payment history is to purchase a big-ticket item on credit and make the minimum monthly payments. While payment history is the greatest factor in your credit score (35% of your FICO score), the way you want to use credit is by making smaller purchases and paying them off quickly.

That's just one suggestion on proper credit utilization. There are so many different ways to save money. I love a good savings challenge but if you have debt, maybe make that savings challenge a debt challenge. Savings is still very important. If these past couple of years have taught us anything (wow….2020 was a couple of years ago!) it's that jobs are scarce, but we make a way even in the face of adversity. Remote jobs are the new normal. Because of this fluid and unsure employment market, saving should always be a priority. We are in a constant state of transition. Life events happen; graduate from high school, college, first job, marriage and kids (if that pertains to you), new home, new car, investments, second careers, and retirement. All of these things happen to everyone. Having money in your savings eases the stress of these major life events.

At some point, something will get in the way of your goal. Prepare for this. If your goal is to pay down $1000 credit card balance or save an extra $1000, give yourself space and grace when it comes to unforeseen circumstances. Understand that the unexpected is out of your control, but what is within your control is the thought process in which you handle it. If you have been diligent with your debt management plan or your savings goals thus far and something unforeseen happens, it's ok to have a setback. Acknowledge how far you have come with your financial goals and accept that you may have to start from scratch. If you started once, you can start again. Stay committed! Now that you have experienced the unforeseen...plan for it the second or third go-around.

Contentment

I'm not sure if you're the type of reader who reads the whole way through in one sitting or if you read a chapter and then take action and come back during each step of the process. Regardless, you have aligned yourself with your goals by this time, committed to redirecting your behavior, and are now aware and better prepared to handle the unexpected. Positive financial behavior is now a daily thought. It may not be daily practice but as I mentioned before, be patient with yourself. Patience and honesty are virtues of finance.

When attempting to reach a goal, one suggestion is to increase income or decrease debt. This is the prime opportunity to see what you have and decide what you are willing to sell. If you are not content with an item and are willing to part with it, think about the time when you purchased it. What did you think? How did you feel? Knowing your thought process from the time of purchase will assist in making more positive financial decisions moving forward. On the other hand, if you forego increasing income and decide to focus on reducing debt, what habits need redirecting to reach these goals?

We all want to reach a point of ease and abundance in our financial situation. This point may come quicker for some than others, and that's ok. When your behaviors align with your goals, abundance and ease will come to all who practice positive financial behavior.

CHAPTER 4

THE JOURNEY: REFLECTION

I love this part of a financial journey because I can remember the exact moment when I started mine. Reflecting on the beginning is such a joyous moment because you can see your highs and lows. You can see how far you came in your journey. You can see the lessons learned from the obstacles that were in the way of your financial journey, and you are now better equipped to create another financial goal. This is when it gets good!

The journey you have started is to help redirect your actions toward positive financial wellness. The way you live your life financially will have an effect on your overall quality of life. Once you go through this process, you can apply this goal-setting method to any goal you set for yourself. Look at your current behaviors, align those behaviors with your goals, take steps toward your goals, ad don't be discouraged by obstacles along the way.

The sacrifices you make now will become easier to transform into positive habits. The hope is that when you look back on what you sacrificed to gain something else, it will be worth it in the end. For example, if someone chose to live off of Ramen Noodles for months so they could pay off their $30,000 student loan debt sooner rather than later, they will look back on that sacrifice, debt-free, and while enjoying a well-deserved steak and lobster dinner. A paid-off debt is an increase in income. You have more money to do with what you want once your debts are paid.

That's the beauty of the journey. Finally getting to that point you promised yourself over and over again, through all of the adversities and excuses. This journey toward your financial goal is uniquely yours and only you can get in your way. You work for your money, you contribute to your savings, you pay your debts, you choose your investments, you keep track of your retirement. Every decision about your money is yours. There is no right or wrong way. There is just your way. Even if this is your halfway point, you can still look back and learn from what you've done so far and make sure you make a note of the exact moment something changed for you for the better. Internalize that moment and continue to put it into practice.

As a financial counselor and educator, I don't compare people and their journeys because, as I mentioned before, each financial plan is unique. Each journey, with all its challenges, is love about financial counseling. I have been able to create action plans for people when they were at the darkest point in their financial situation. No matter how impossible you think it is, with a good plan, there is always a way. If you arm yourself with information, commitment, and a plan, you can redirect your past behaviors into positive ones without a shadow of a doubt.

When I learned the order in which I needed to direct my finances, that's the point in my journey when I realized that my positive behaviors and small sacrifices were working. I remember when I went to work and sat with the financial counselor at my office to learn a little bit more about the finance life, he asked me, "What is this money in your savings for?" My answer was that it was for an emergency fund. Then the counselor looked at my debts (which was just my credit card) and my expenses (which were also very minimal because we lived on base in Germany at the time), and he informed me that I had way more than necessary in my savings. I immediately transferred money to my credit card and stayed with only $500 in my savings. I'm not going to lie, this was very uncomfortable for me, but it was probably the best decision. I managed to pay off the rest of my credit card debt within months by changing my variable expenses. I made coffee and breakfast at home rather than eating out, which helped significantly. Once I paid off my debt, I focused on savings. I saved $10,000 from January to May on a $33k salary and two children. Since I didn't have any debts to pay and minimal expenses (daycare was my biggest expense), my focus was savings. I was able to pay my half of their daycare and school expenses without worry or anxiety. I started with a $9k in credit card debt and a $7k car payment. Three years later, I was debt-free and had significant savings to cover the expenses for an international military move. I did it my way. I didn't need to buy into a class or a program, and I didn't need to see how someone else was doing it. I just learned from a financial counselor, shifted my financial behavior, and made small sacrifices. The journey was mine and I enjoyed every bit of it.

Tackling debt.

There are so many outside factors that we can "blame" for our lack of understanding of personal finance. For example, it wasn't taught in school or at home for some. Some grew up during the recession when the economy was unstable. BUT, you can also pinpoint certain behaviors that have led to frivolous spending that stops you from reaching your goals. The great thing about identifying this behavior is that you can redirect it! You have no control over the lack of financial education, but you can educate yourself now.

If you feel you need a loan, an advance, or some other form of financial assistance to kick start your financial journey, I highly recommend speaking to a financial counselor first to create a plan. Personal loans may be a quick fix for immediate relief, but please consider developing a plan without the loan first and then create one with the loan included. If time is of the essence, and you need immediate assistance, contact a financial counselor afterward to create a repayment plan.

Being in a not-so-great place financially is not always bad; it can be an opportunity to align, redirect, and go through the journey.

What are the examples of small sacrifices that someone might make on this journey?

Here are a few examples of small sacrifices that someone might make on this journey:

-Driving a used older fuel-efficient vehicle, even though you would prefer to have a newer vehicle. If you have a newer car in mind, create a plan, save up enough to make manageable payments within your financial means.

-Reduce the number of variable expenses you can control, such as going out to dinner and shopping. Or sell stuff to increase income. Letting things go can be just much of a sacrifice as not spending.

-Eating leftovers for lunch instead of going out to eat even though you can afford it. Meal prep or carry $10 cash; once that money for the week is up, you can't eat out.

The idea is that you want to do everything possible to make better financial decisions that align yourself with your goal. The great thing is that these sacrifices are temporary, and once you have reached your goals, you can either go back and spend as you wish because you now have more disposable income.

So up until this point, we have identified our behaviors, aligned our behaviors with our goals, committed to our decision to practice positive financial behaviors, and accepted that small sacrifices might need to happen, but they are temporary. I'm sure you feel some relief by this point, even though you still have some time until you have reached the end. You may be at the beginning of your journey, you may have a long way to go, or you may be very close to the end. Either way, you should be proud of yourself by this point. Give yourself some kudos!

Regression… happens to everyone.

If you find yourself regressing into old habits, think about what's at stake if you act on this previous behavior. Think about how you would truly feel if you acted on impulse or emotion. That feeling of gratification is short-lived. Then think about how you would feel if you were one step closer to achieving your goal. It's not to say you can't have the desire to spend the money or act on the desire to spend the money, but think about how it aligns with your goals or maybe even a way to make the purchase still and reach your goal simultaneously. If you are aware that this behavior is not in line with your goals or if making the decision is detrimental to your income, sleep on it and find a more positive way to approach the situation.

In reality, the feeling of acting on impulse may come from fear. Fear that you won't reach your financial goal, so you might as well buy all of this now, right? Take a moment to address your financial worries and how you manage your concerns by applying what you've learned in previous chapters. This could be as simple as spending 5 minutes visualizing the worst-case scenario, but it's also important to remember this fear may be the reason why you haven't been able to reach your financial goals when you have set them in the past. Thinking about the worst-case scenarios might bring back those fears, but if you spend time thinking about the consequences of not making a change, you'll probably fear those consequences as well.

CHAPTER 5

FINANCIAL ENLIGHTENMENT/REVELATION

Financial enlightenment is the point in your journey when you feel that weight lifting and your redirected behaviors come with less effort. It's that point where you have that a-ha moment with the deep exhale. As I mentioned in chapter 4, the only thing you have complete control over are your finances. You make the choice to put your money where your goal is. Enlightenment will happen and your funds will reveal themselves to be abundant, regardless of your salary. I have two kids and had a $33k salary. My moment of enlightenment was when I made my last debt payment (besides my student loans which I wasn't playing at the time due to the Covid hold) and realized that my next check was all mine. It fell in the middle of the month and all my bills were paid at the beginning of the month. I didn't owe anybody anything. When I received my paycheck in the middle of the month, it was all disposable income. What I had done worked. I was enlightened.

Do you feel fulfilled?

"A big part of financial freedom is having your heart and mind free from worry about the what-ifs of life" – Suze Orman

Now that we have a slight understanding about putting value to every dollar, we have more respect for the dollars we make and a better grasp on where it is best placed for our financial goals. Being free of worry is more about being better prepared. The more prepared you are financial, the better you can handle the unforeseen circumstances and the less stress you have when it does arrive. An increase in your salary will not give you financial freedom until you redirect your behaviors in a more positive direction.

This is the time to feel enlightened about your financial journey but ask yourself if you feel fulfilled. If you don't feel fulfilled even though what you're doing is working, you are not working toward the goal you truly want. If you realize that you're paying down your debt and don't feel fulfilled, ask yourself why? It might be time to go back and realign, or maybe you're just not motivated at the moment.

If your financial connection is emotionally driven (you experience highs and lows when you spend money), you may tend to get a sense of false fulfillment, which may be why your goal isn't allowing you to feel that fulfilled. Your financial goal may not be monetary. Since your attachment to money could be emotional (such as fear, impulse, or stress), setting goals to pay off debt or save will not fulfill you until you tackle these personal triggers.

It is worth mentioning that a financial behavior specialist or a financial counselor can assist in these situations. Your connection to money may be emotional. You'd rather not deal with money because it's either too stressful. So you push away anything finance-related so that you don't have to deal with it. With all of this, having financial freedom and reaching that a-ha moment is not out of reach. You might find fulfillment in speaking to a financial behavior specialist or a financial counselor as your goal.

Give, and it will be given to you. A good measure, pressed down, shaken together, and running over, will be poured into your lap. For with the measure you use, it will be measured to you – Luke 6:38

Learning about personal finance can be incredibly empowering

The more you learn about personal finance, the more you want to learn. You may also notice that the more you know, the less likely you are to fall into your old financial behaviors. My goal is to plant a tiny seed of financial inspiration so that you can go and research what financial information you can use for your goals. There is a wealth of information at your disposal. Savings challenges are useful if used with a grain of salt. They don't account for the unexpected, evaluate your income and debt/expenses, and don't know your financial habits. The more you read and learn about different savings methods, the better equipped you are to look at your income, your debts and expenses, and create your own savings plan to reach your goals. Savings apps that charge, even if it is $2 or $4 or $10 bucks, aren't necessary if you take the time to learn how to budget, learn more about your interest rates, and set up a good plan.

I don't want you to give up when you feel overwhelmed by all of the information out there. I know there is a lot! Most of the information regarding personal finance is almost the same. When you are looking for a podcast or audiobook to listen to, it's best to find something that resonates with you. Different people have varying learning styles, so think about how you learn best before searching for financial information. Are you a hands-on learner? Visual learner? Do you learn best by listening? The same goes for this book! If the information provided does not align with your goals, I promise there is something out there that is a good fit for you. The only thing I want to urge you against is learning misinformation. If it looks or sounds gimmicky, then it probably is.

Learning about personal finance can be incredibly enlightening and empowering, but only if it fits in your life. This book is about taking your old habits and redirecting them. If you learn something about finances that assists in developing your positive financial behavior, keep nurturing that behavior. All you need is a little seed of information and patience with yourself to see financial growth.

There are a lot of myths and misconceptions about money that need debunking

One of the main ones I believe is the most useful is credit usage. Many people think they have to buy something on credit and make the minimum payments each month to show good credit usage and payment history. While late payments do affect your credit score negatively, making the minimum payment on a large balance isn't the way to prove good payment history. The best way to show good credit utilization and payment history is to make small purchases each month on your credit card that you are able to pay off once the transaction posts to your account. This way, you are not paying any interest on items you purchase. Making the minimum payment or paying a little extra on something you have to pay down monthly accrues interest. For example, if you buy a $400 item and make minimum payments plus a little extra over the next few months, you are still paying interest. So you will end up paying $450 or more for that $400 tv because of the interest. So, credit is for small payments just to get the credit utilization and payment history you need to boost your credit score. You can put big-ticket items on credit IF you have saved up enough to transfer the money to pay it off, but if you're not very good at keeping track of charges on your card or you charge too much on your credit card, then maybe this is the behavior we want to redirect.

Investing is another area of finance that people "fear" because they are not informed enough. Many people think you need a lot of money to start investing and reap the benefits. Additionally, people aren't risk-takers so investing seems too risky. However, there are ways to invest very little and enjoy long-term benefits, and you don't have to just invest in the volatile stock market. You also don’t need to pay an advisor lots of money to start investing. You can do this for free, on your own, from the comfort of your home if you just do a little research or talk to a financial counselor and learn the pure basics.

One thing that breaks my heart about others' financial journeys is when they make comparisons. You might feel that the only way to get to a point financially as someone else who has the same goal is to do exactly what they did. This is not the case. Maybe you can learn from some methods they used, but mimicking everything they did may not get you to the same point in the same amount of time. This will lead to feelings of frustration, like you've failed at reaching your goal and you absolutely have not. You haven't failed. You just have to do what works best for you.

It might be that your thought process about money is what needs to be redirected. We mentioned the emotional connection earlier, but your mental connection may be why you aren't fulfilled in your financial journey. What you think about money or the lack of financial knowledge may be what's deterring you from formulating financial goals. You want to invest but don't know where to start, so you just don't. If this is you, learning from a financial counselor or a well-sourced podcast or book might help. I have had a good bit of clients who believe they "know" about personal finance, but when it's time to create an action plan for their goals, they realize that what they know doesn't work for them. Your mental and emotional connections to money and finance should be something worth talking to someone about so that you can reach your financial goals and feel that enlightened moment. Willingness to learn and receive advice is imperative for those with a mental disconnect regarding money.

Along with a financial counselor to speak to one-on-one, a solid support system is imperative for your mental and emotional wellbeing throughout the financial journey. If you start to better your situation by reducing the amount of "fun" you have and realize that your circle is getting smaller, this may be for the better. Your finances are very personal, but having a support system that you confide in can make the journey a little less stressful and maybe even more fun!

It's necessary to surround yourself with a supportive community

Positive financial decisions come from a place of passion. If your heart is not in the right place when it comes to your finances, you'll have a tough time following through on what might be best for you and your family. It is necessary to surround yourself with a supportive community that will support you along your journey. Mentors are also a great way to stay on track and credible resources to learn from as you navigate.

I remember when I started, I met with a financial counselor regularly. It helped that we worked in the same office, so this may be to your advantage if your employer has an in-office financial counselor. I learned so much from sitting with the financial counselor and picking his brain. I developed a craving for financial information. Any methods or concepts I learned, I researched and applied them to my life. My journey was full of enlightening moments because I learned things that weren't taught in school or at home. Even now, as a financial counselor and financial education instructor, I have a mentor and am still learning so much. I went from not having any financial knowledge, starting on a journey toward positive financial behaviors, and somewhere along the way, I took it way too far and made it my livelihood. My passion for educating others and ensuring that they know they can reach their financial goals is what motivates me every day. To do this, I needed a support system. Even though they didn't know my exact financial situation, my friends cheered me on. They saw my journey and growth and still supported me while I learned who I was as a future financial counselor. I started a budget book club to inform my circle about what I learned through my studies and sessions with a financial counselor.

CHAPTER 6

FINDING PEACE, REJOICING, AND EXPRESSIONS OF GRATITUDE

Once you have aligned your goals with your behaviors and have had your eyes opened to the fact that it's working, you naturally come to this place of exhausting. When you make that last payment, or you see the number you have strived to reach in your savings account, or you sign the papers on a home or business, it's natural to take a step back, but you absolutely can't help that happy dance. That's the moment you rejoice, and then you say a million thank yous to friends and family members who may have held you accountable along the way. And then you sit down after your celebration and take that deep exhale, you are now at peace. All that stuff is behind you.

Celebrating the big win is such an amazing feeling, but it's good to celebrate the little wins also. The time you didn't let any obstacle get in your way. That time you reached your quarter of the way or the halfway mark. No matter how big or small your accomplishments are, take some time out of each day to celebrate them. This could be as simple as taking 15 minutes at the end of the day to reflect on all the positive things that happened, or it could be as involved as taking a day-long retreat. The one thing I want to avoid is omitting the things you love. Do them! So long as you do them with your goals in mind and a realistic account of your finances. If you reach a milestone in your journey and maybe someone helped you along the way, take them out to eat or spend the day doing something they want. Celebrate and keep yourself happy. I honestly don't believe money buys happiness but not having money troubles certainly makes everyone happy!

In the same way that finding peace with your finances can help you avoid stress, rejoicing in those same accomplishments will allow you to appreciate what makes you happy on a more intimate level. If your financial situation isn't bringing you peace at this point, you can rejoice in the little wins, and it's time to evaluate HOW you are making money. If your job isn't for you, then slowly start making the transition toward doing what you love to do that will also bring you income; keyword, slowly. Make sure it makes financial sense to make that transition.

I feel incredibly blessed to have a full-time job as a financial counselor. Doing this allows me to inform, educate, and continuously learn about what makes me happy, which in turn has brought me on the path of writing this book. Once you find your passion, and your passion brings revenue, you'll be more inclined to think about where every dollar goes because that's happy money! You want to make happy money! When you're happy, your financial situation becomes more positive. And naturally, your behaviors become more positive.

Personal Finance is a tool.

Many people have gotten very wealthy by creating classes and programs about getting your finances in order. Do this savings strategy to reach your goal, this is how to properly budget, starve yourself to pay off debt! Although I have done the ramen noodle lunch diet, it's not for everybody. Not many people take the time to think about the person who set the goal. It's disheartening to see clients who have tried every program and they keep ending up at square one. It's because those programs are like diets and what you need is to redirect your behavior. They call it a "lifestyle change in the exercise and nutrition world." You need a finance-style change. You can't do the same financial diet everyone else is doing and expect the same results. So what would YOUR diet be? Meal prep your finances. Plan it out and make it fun. Use the tools available to you to create your own financial workout plan.

If you have started redirecting your behavior and you got just a smidge closer to your goal than you were last time, celebrate and rejoice in that! Nothing is stopping you from taking yourself further than you ever imagined possible. Keep it up and make it a habit. Positive financial behaviors should also be considered, and probably re-evaluated, when there is a life-changing event such as an engagement, a new baby, or the purchase of a home. Embrace these new moments in your life because you have now prepared yourself mentally and monetarily to tackle these hurdles. You have started with smaller goals which are just stepping stones to larger goals. Now you can look back at the smaller challenges such as that check engine light and smile because you overcame that challenge, you stayed committed to your goal, and you are now rejoicing in your outcome. You are equipped with tools in your financial toolbox to go for bigger and better.

When it comes down to it, personal finance is a tool and how you use this tool to build your financial goals is entirely up to you. The more time and effort you put into learning how to make more informed decisions with your finances, the further away you get from the burdens and struggles of the past. This is why it's so important to focus on the positive behaviors and small wins, even when there aren't any results to show for it yet. It might take weeks or months before you start seeing the differences of these new choices, but eventually, you will reap the benefits and rejoice. So be patient with yourself and proud of yourself!

Embrace the journey, not the destination

It helps to focus on the destination because your end goal may change or get pushed back, which might discourage you. Instead, embrace the journey and realize that patience is a virtue. You don't want to put in all that effort only to give up halfway through just because you didn't reach where you wanted to be right away. If you consider the journey to be more important than reaching your destination, you won't lose motivation when bad things happen or you encounter setbacks. This is when your support system is needed the most. For some, your love language is words of affirmation, your support system can speak the words you need to encourage you. On the other hand, your love language may be action, so sitting with your support system to create a new plan might be what you need to feel motivated. Then, when you reach a point toward the end of your journey, you can look back and be proud that you overcame that small moment of dissatisfaction.

Success is subjective and completely dependent on how committed someone is. When you want something badly enough, hard work and persistence will seem a little more effortless as time goes on. The bigger your aspirations are, the harder you have to work. Suppose you have big dreams of owning a business or opening a practice/firm, creating something bigger than yourself for yourself. In that case, it helps to put positive financial behaviors into practice with all the information you have learned thus far. But with all your big dreams, please remember to be patient with yourself. Having big dreams is fantastic, but it's not as fun when the journey toward it brings you stress and not peace.

Do not let challenges kill your joy!

We all face setbacks from time to time--that's just part of life. But, when challenges come up that might prevent us from achieving our next primary financial goal, it's important to stay positive and work your way through them. Remember, this is your journey so you are in control. You are in control of your emotions and your mental space. You know how much you can handle. When the unexpected happens and a wrench is thrown in your plans, take a minute to pause and think. You have gotten to a point in your financial journey where you have aligned, committed, you've practiced discipline, and have experienced that enlightening moment. You have your joy and peace. That moment, at the very end, when you're so close to your goal- that's when your tenacity matters the most.

When challenges present themselves, we tend to have discouraging thoughts about ourselves as well as our inability to handle the situation. If my financial journey has taught me anything, no challenge shall prosper if you have a good plan. There is no obstacle you can't overcome. Give yourself some time to think about a few solutions and what might be the best financial course of action for each solution. The one that makes the most sense financially and still allows you to achieve your goal in the same amount of time is best. The second option is the one that makes sense and has the least impact on your goal. If a complete revamp is required, then so be it, but stay focused because you and your goals are a priority.

Practice gratitude every day

"Be thankful for what you have; you'll end up having more. If you concentrate on what you don't have, you will never, ever, have enough" – Oprah Winfrey

I'm not sure what your spiritual belief is, but I am a firm believer in energy. The energy you put out is the energy you will receive. Being kind, expressing gratitude, and positive thinking are at the forefront of my daily actions. Positive thinking can be tough when you are in the thick of a financial situation. My suggestion would be to only look to the past for things that worked and be thankful that there is always the future to look forward to. As long as there is tomorrow, something can be done about your financial circumstances today.

Don't forget to thank yourself! You made it this far in your financial journey. Thank yourself for being willing to learn and stepping out of your previous financial behavior and into a positive behavior.

Actively express gratitude to your support system. They are the ones going through this journey with you in one form or another, with nothing to gain financially. They just want to see you win and achieve your goals. What can you do for them to show them you are grateful?

What does gratitude mean to you? For some, it's "I'm so glad my car didn't break down today!" That is something to be very grateful for! If you don't have a car, be grateful for public transportation, taxis, and Uber and Lyft. You are still able to get around. Bikes and legs all of a sudden become very underrated. When you, at minimum, have a gracious mind, your body starts to feel lighter, and things just fall into place.

Gratitude is important because it allows us to recognize how much we have accomplished through our efforts and relationships with others, rather than always focusing on what is still left to do. So, try to make it a habit of going through your daily life with gratitude and a positive attitude. This doesn't mean go out and say thank you to everyone for everything! Start with yourself, and then when you genuinely feel grateful for something someone did for you, you can turn a "Thanks!" into "I appreciate your help." Doing so will make your journey towards smart financial decision-making more meaningful and help refuel you along the way. How you express yourself, verbal and non-verbal, coincides with your thought process. Words and actions are powerful.

So remember to rejoice, embrace this new peace over your financial situation, and show yourself some gratitude. Do this daily and your journey, and how to tackle difficult situations, will get easier.

CHAPTER 7

COMING FULL CIRCLE....AND BEGINNING AGAIN.

The best way to achieve the goals you want in your life is by taking things one step at a time. Since we will never know it all, always be open to opportunities and new information that may challenge your current way of thinking and help you improve with your money management skills. Having a positive outlook and staying committed to your goals will help you reach them, so don't lose sight of what's important in your life. And, focus on making positive financial decisions with the money you have today; celebrate both your successes and challenges along the way, and be grateful for all you have accomplished.

Making positive financial decisions is possible for anyone who takes the time to reflect on their tendencies, align them with your goals, and make a shift if they don't align. Hopefully, this guide has helped you see your behaviors more clearly and provided you with some ideas about redirecting your habits for the better. We all have room for improvement in our finances, so don't be too hard on yourself if you find that the shift or the sacrifices are difficult at first. Just start small and take things one step at a time; before you know it, you'll be well on your way to a more prosperous future.

I hope this guide has helped you reflect on your financial decisions and given you some tools to make positive choices in the future. Making minor tweaks to your spending habits can have a significant impact down the line, so do not be afraid to experiment a little and find what works best for you. Remember, there is no one-size-fits-all solution for personal finance; what works for someone else may not work for you. The most important thing is to take a step back, assess your situation honestly, and develop a plan that will help you reach your financial goals.

In addition, it is never too late to start making better financial decisions – all it takes is a bit of self-reflection and determination.

The most important takeaway is that although this is the end of one journey toward your goal, there will be more goals to set and more things to achieve. Positive financial behaviors are a constant work in progress, but I do not doubt that you can master your behaviors and improve your finances. Even when you come full circle, you are actually starting over with a better understanding of self and newfound confidence. I hope I have motivated you to take control of your behaviors or, at minimum, seek assistance from a financial counselor in your area that can create a plan with you. A financial counselor or a finance behavior specialist will be able to identify areas of improvement, talk about your attachment to money, and the best ways to achieve your goals.

Thank you for reading my book, and I am honestly so excited about your financial journey. I'm a pretty average person, so if my book has helped in any way, I'd love to hear from you!

Debbie J. Slaughter

Made in United States
North Haven, CT
04 November 2026

21765357R00035